King's Things

An Adult Coloring Book For Men

by Dan Greene

Dedication

To Vince

Acknowledgements

Some of the images in this book were modified under Creative Commons License 3.0. A link to the license is provided here:
creativecommons.org/licenses/by/3.0
Special thanks to Lorc and Delapoutie.

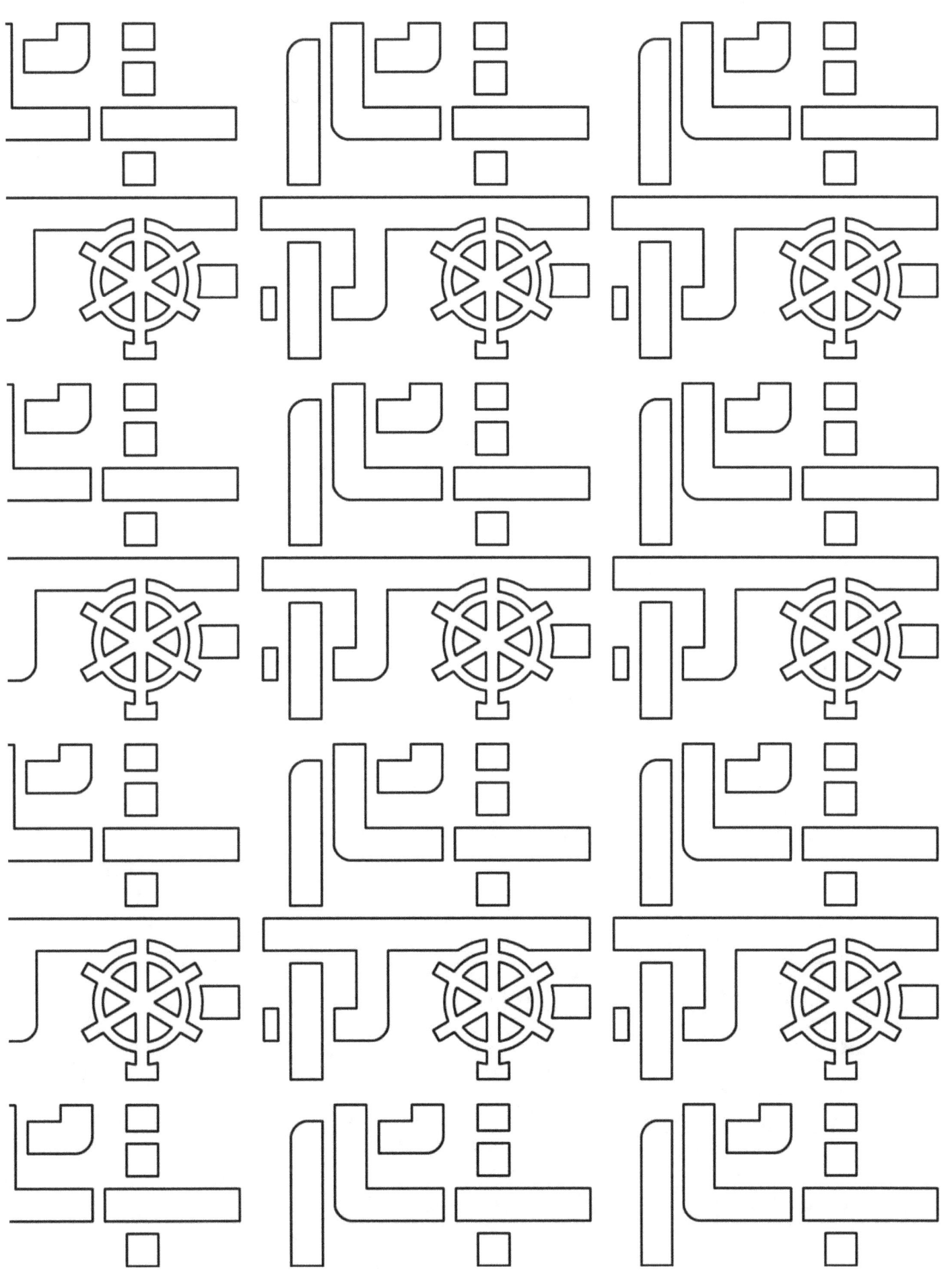

Notes

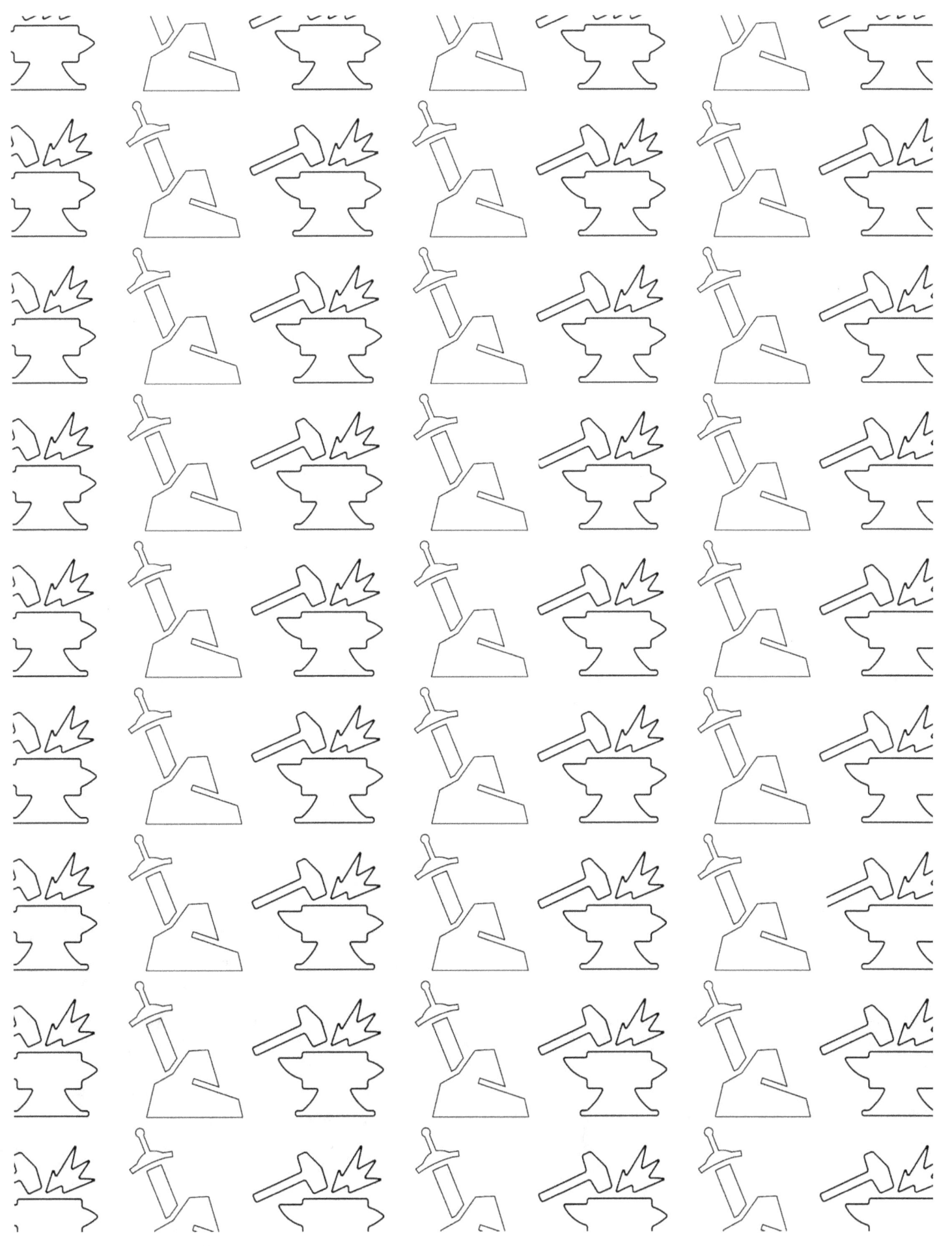

Notes

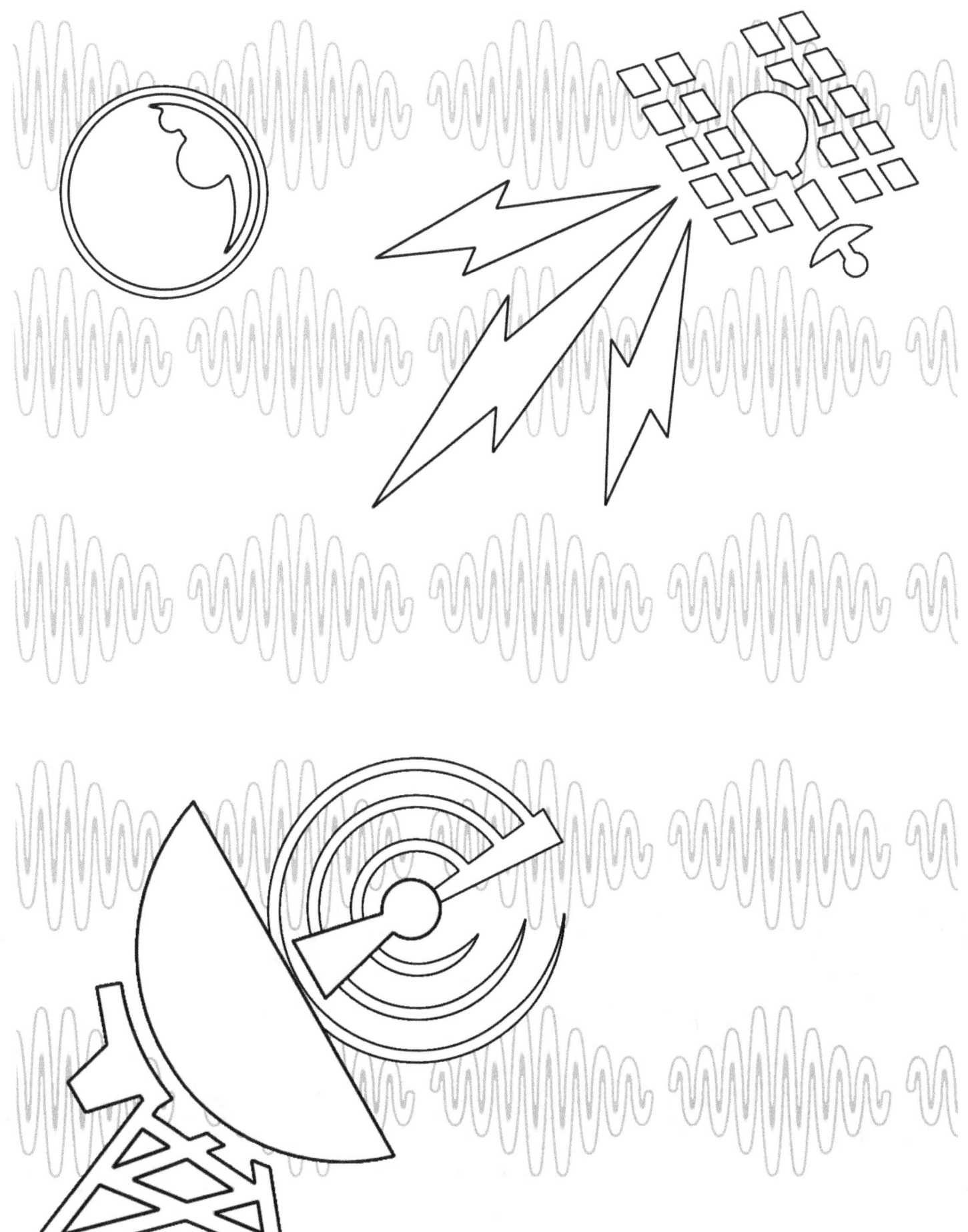

Notes

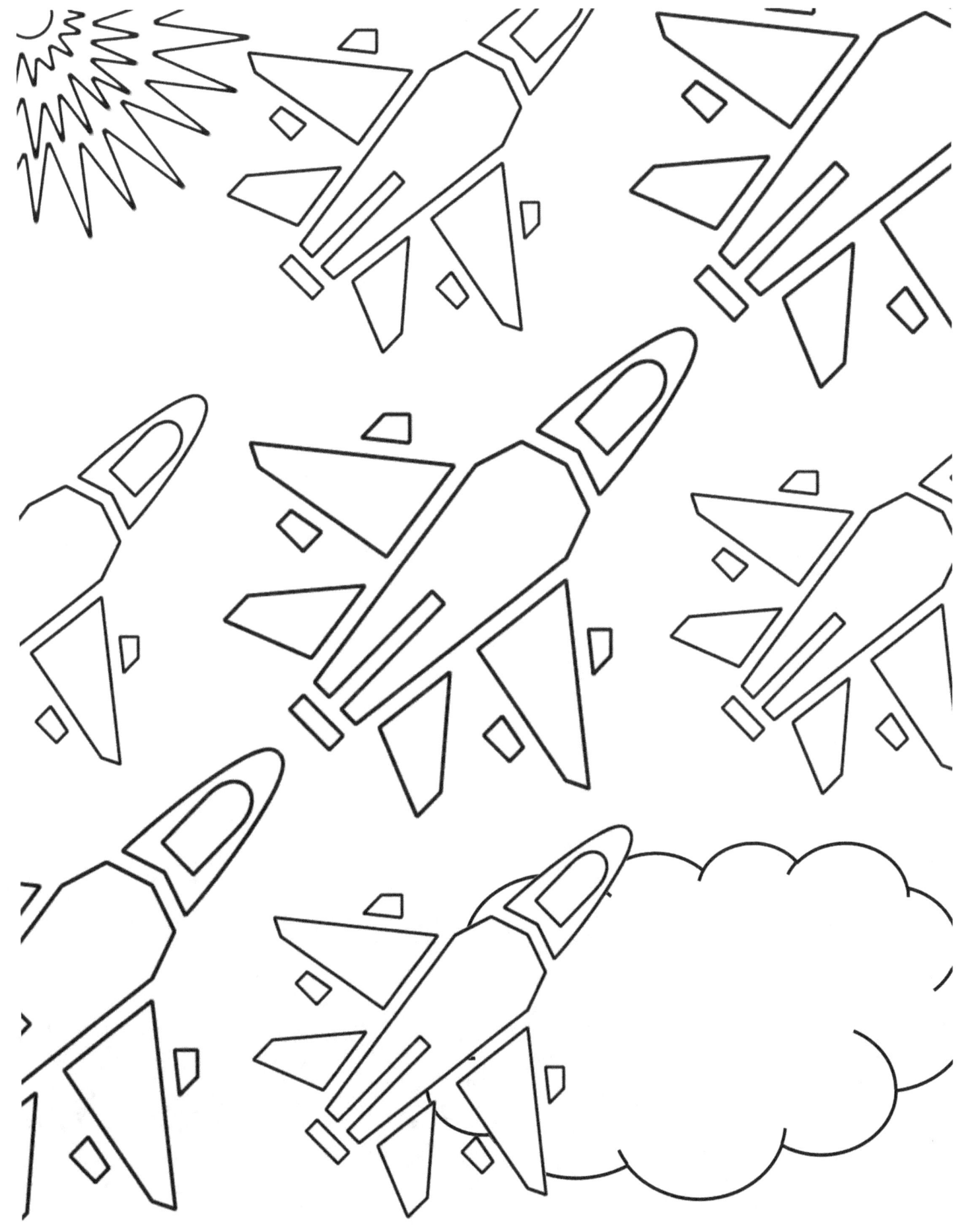

Notes

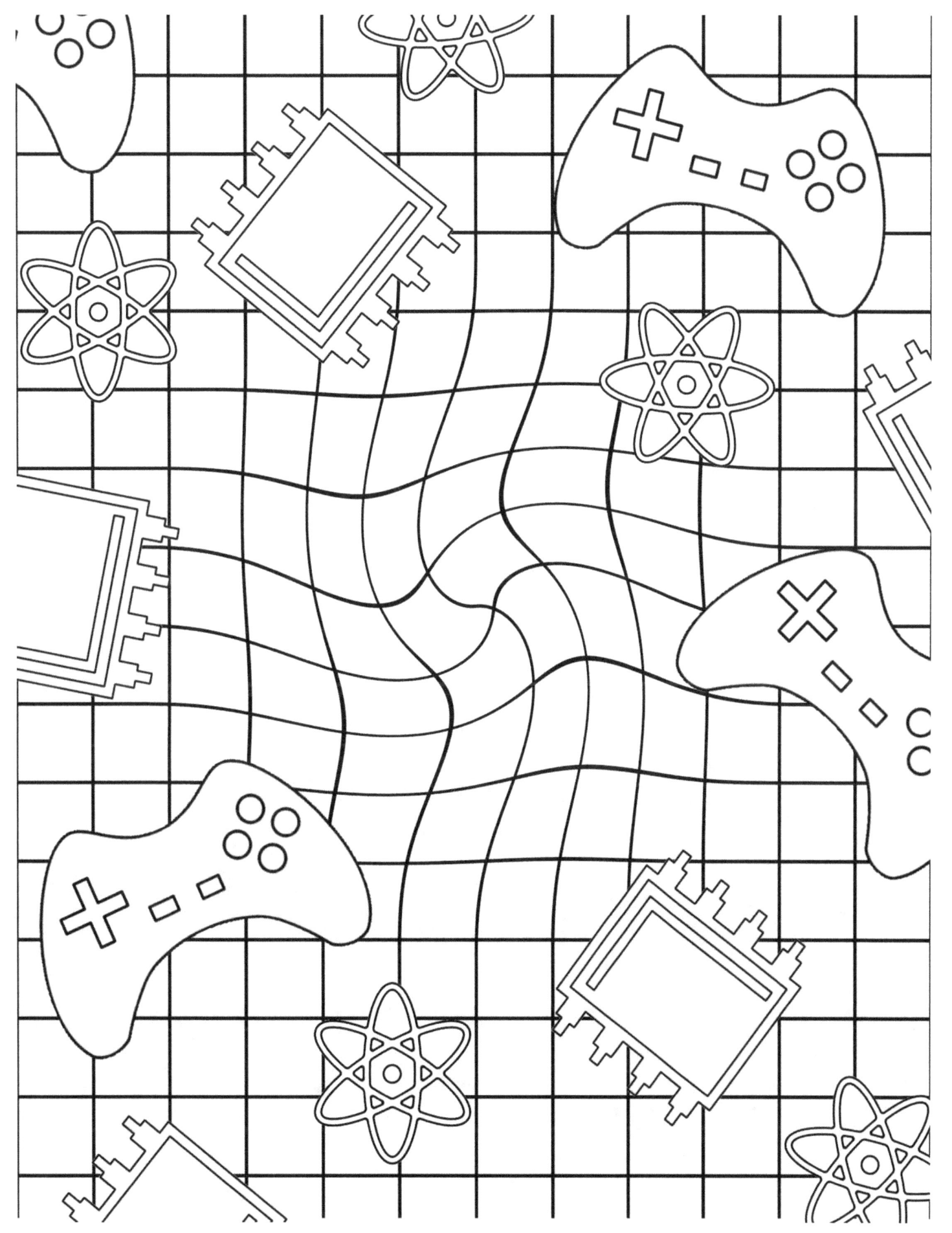

Notes

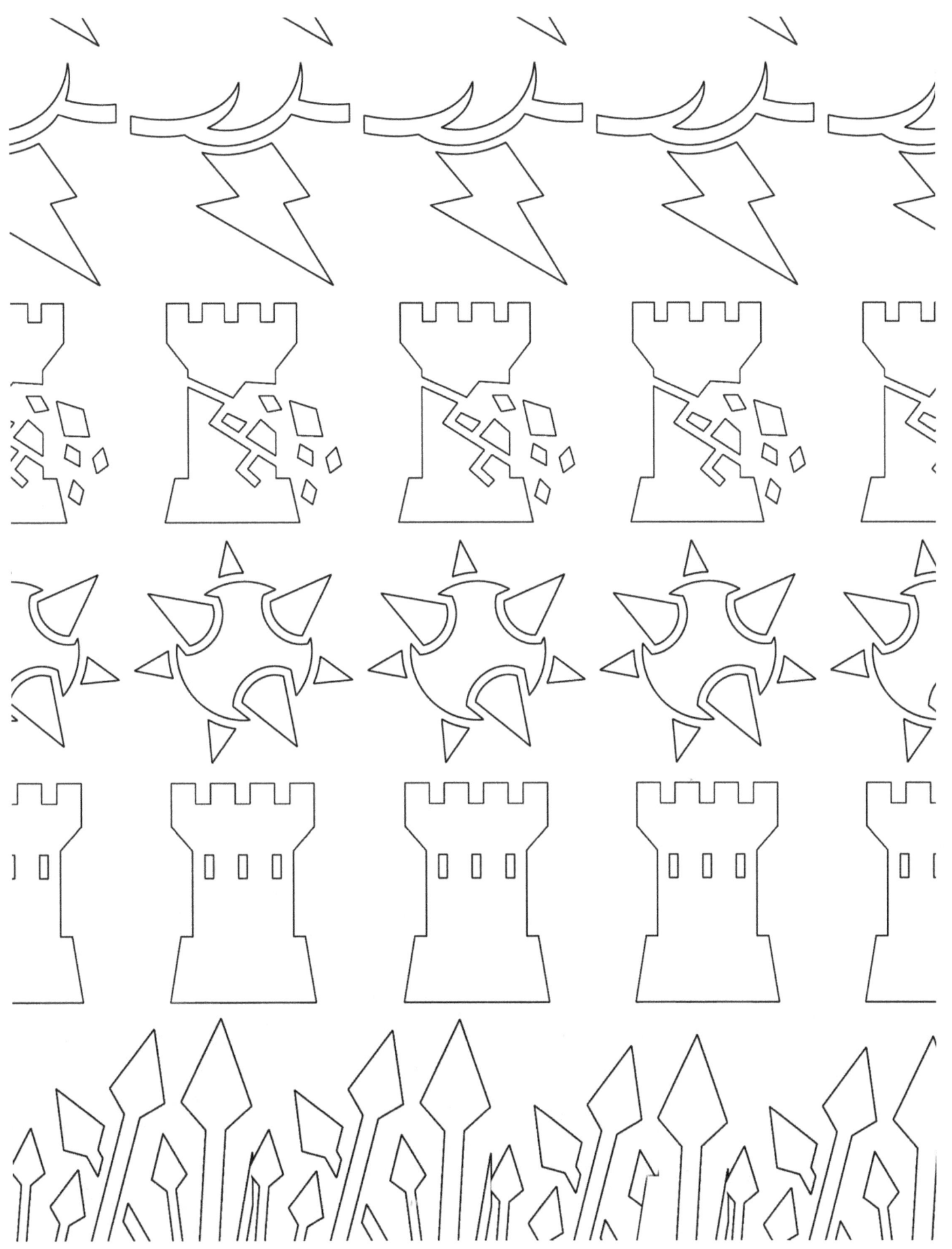

Notes

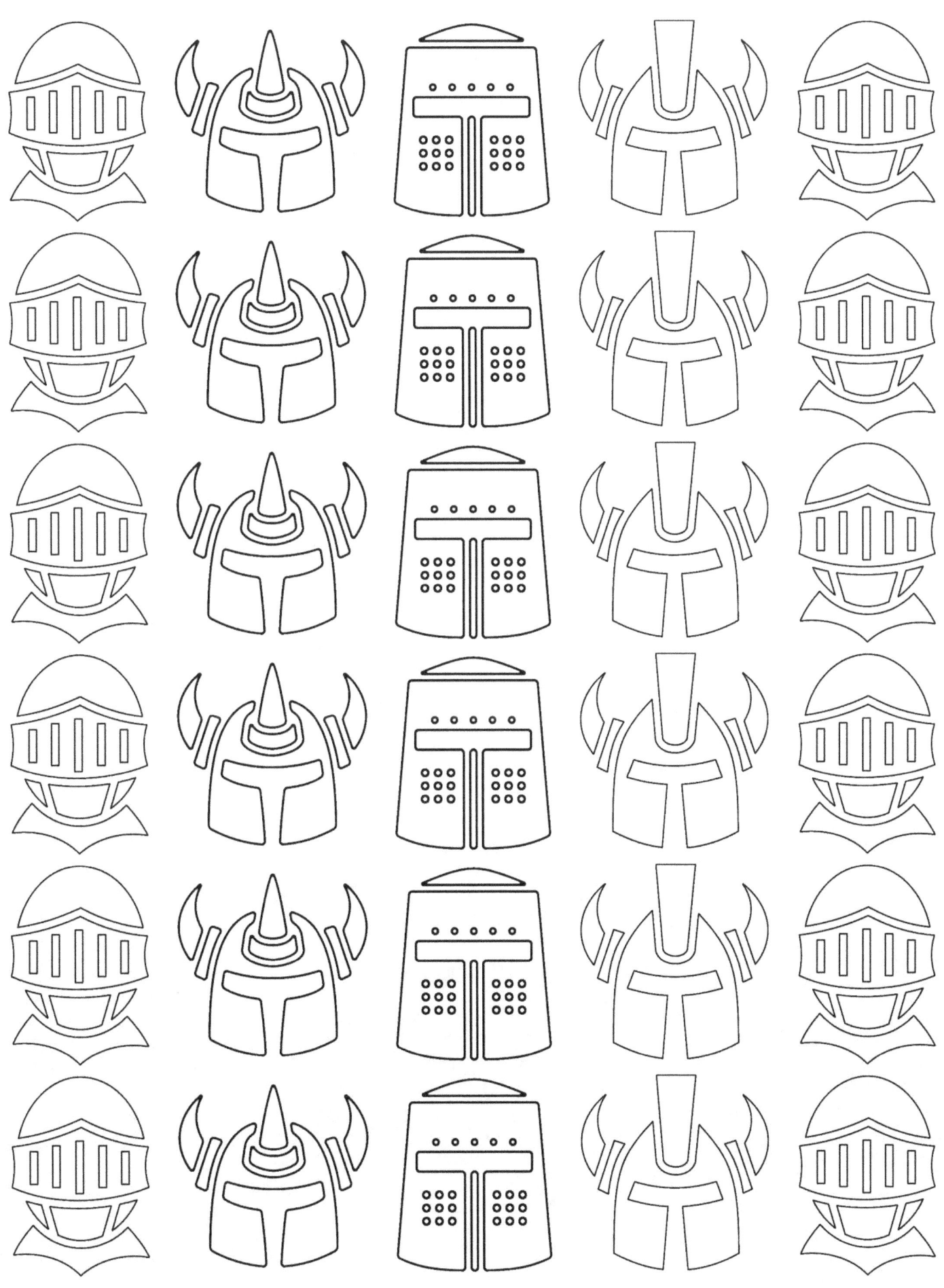

Notes

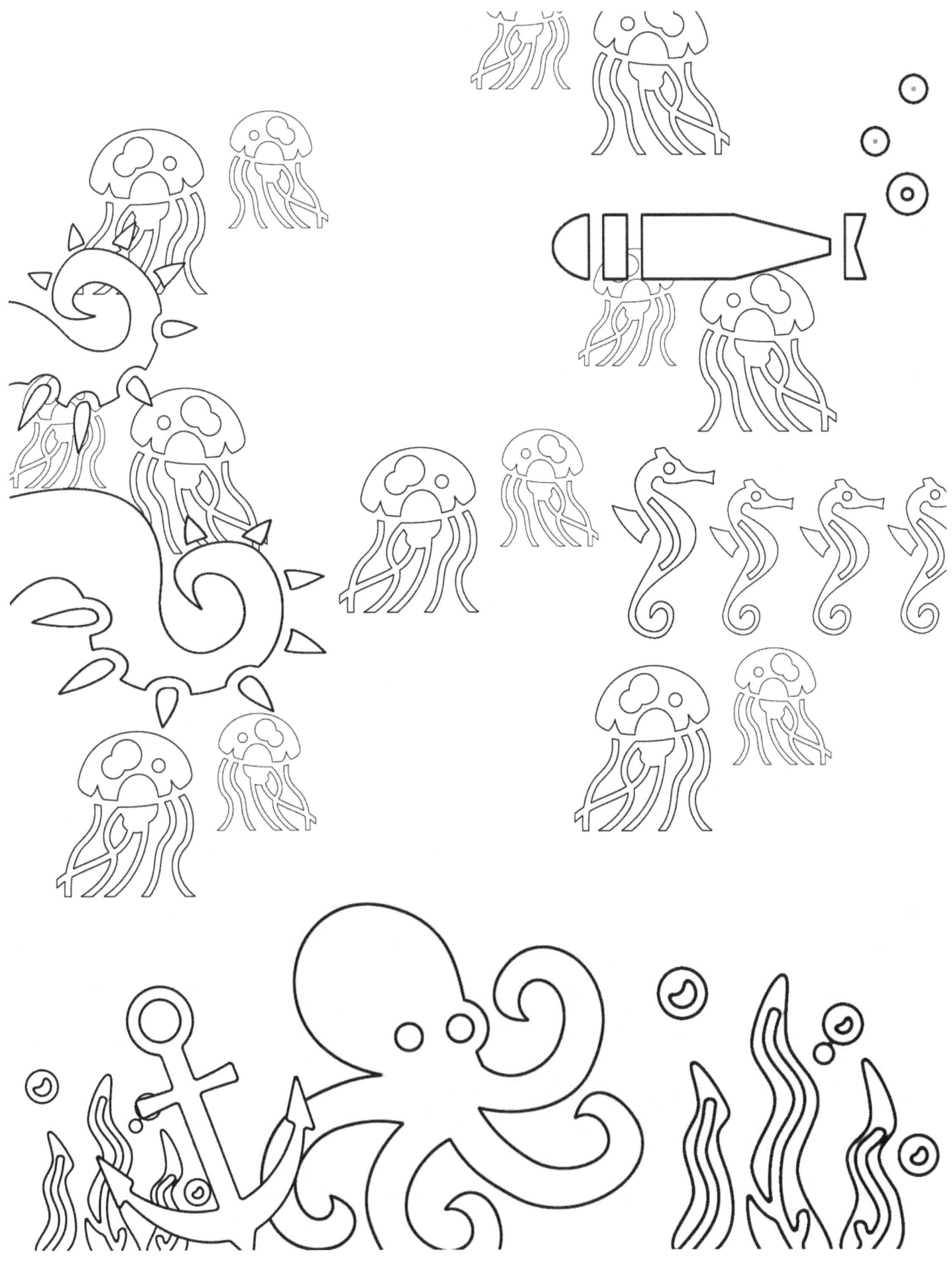

Notes

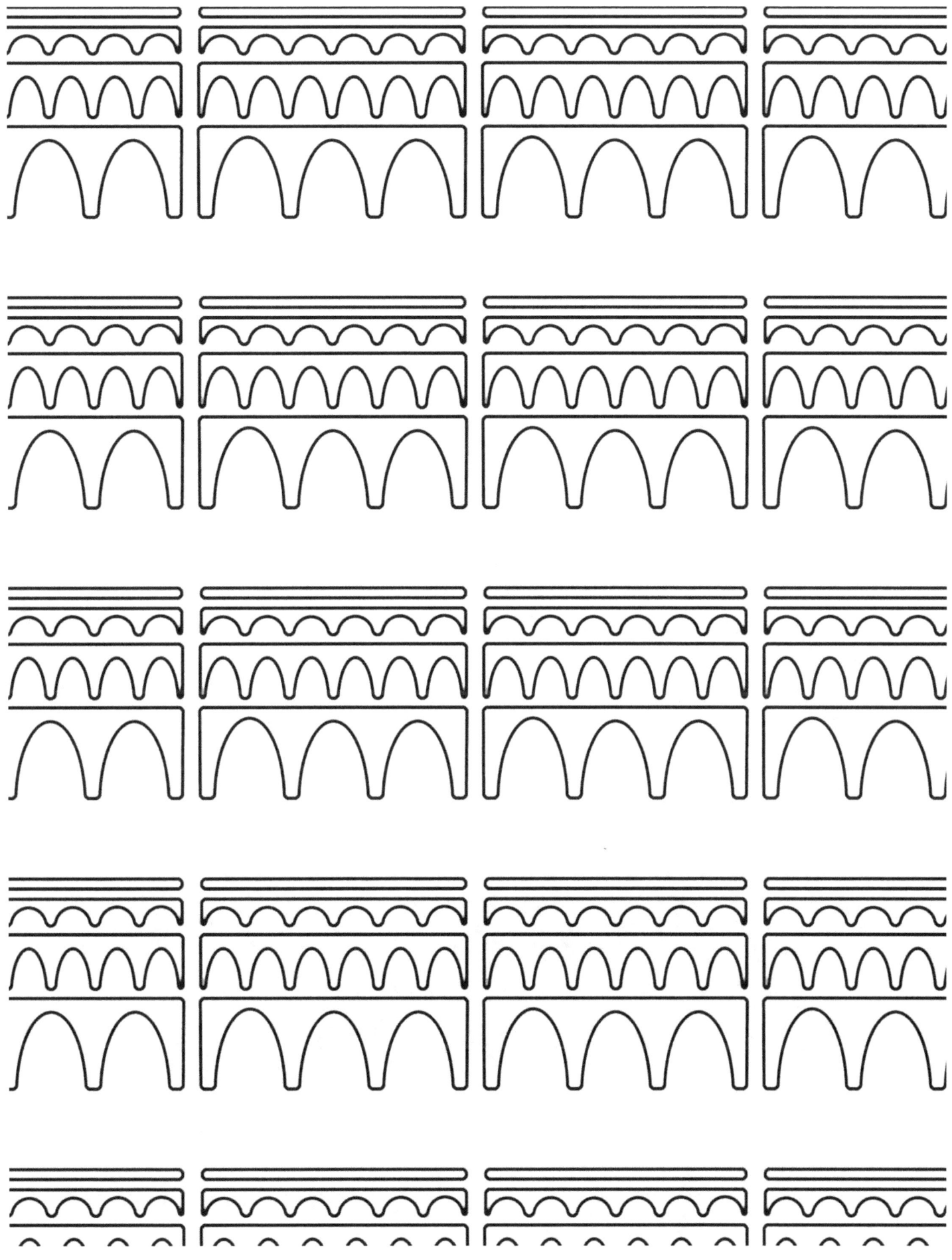

Notes

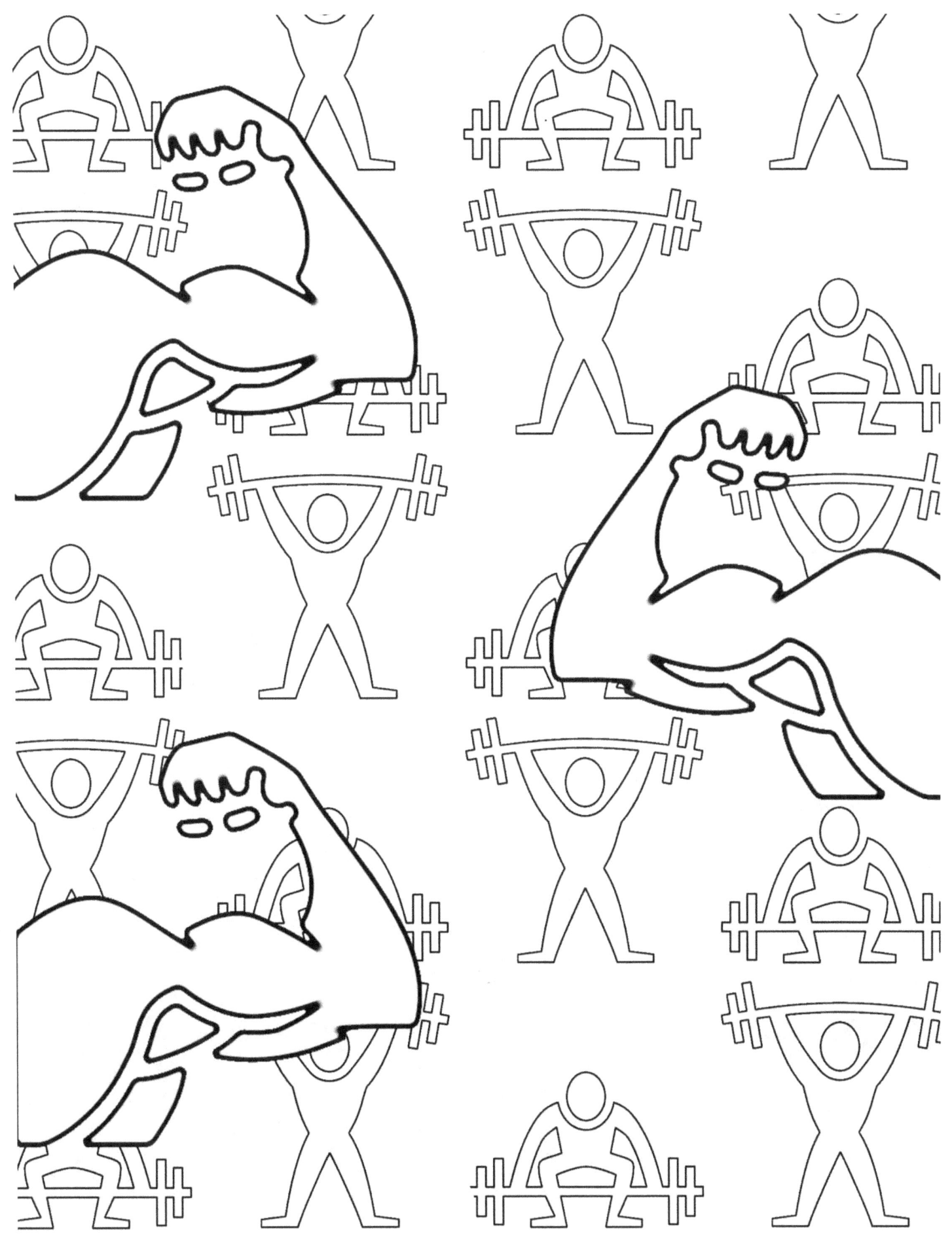

Notes

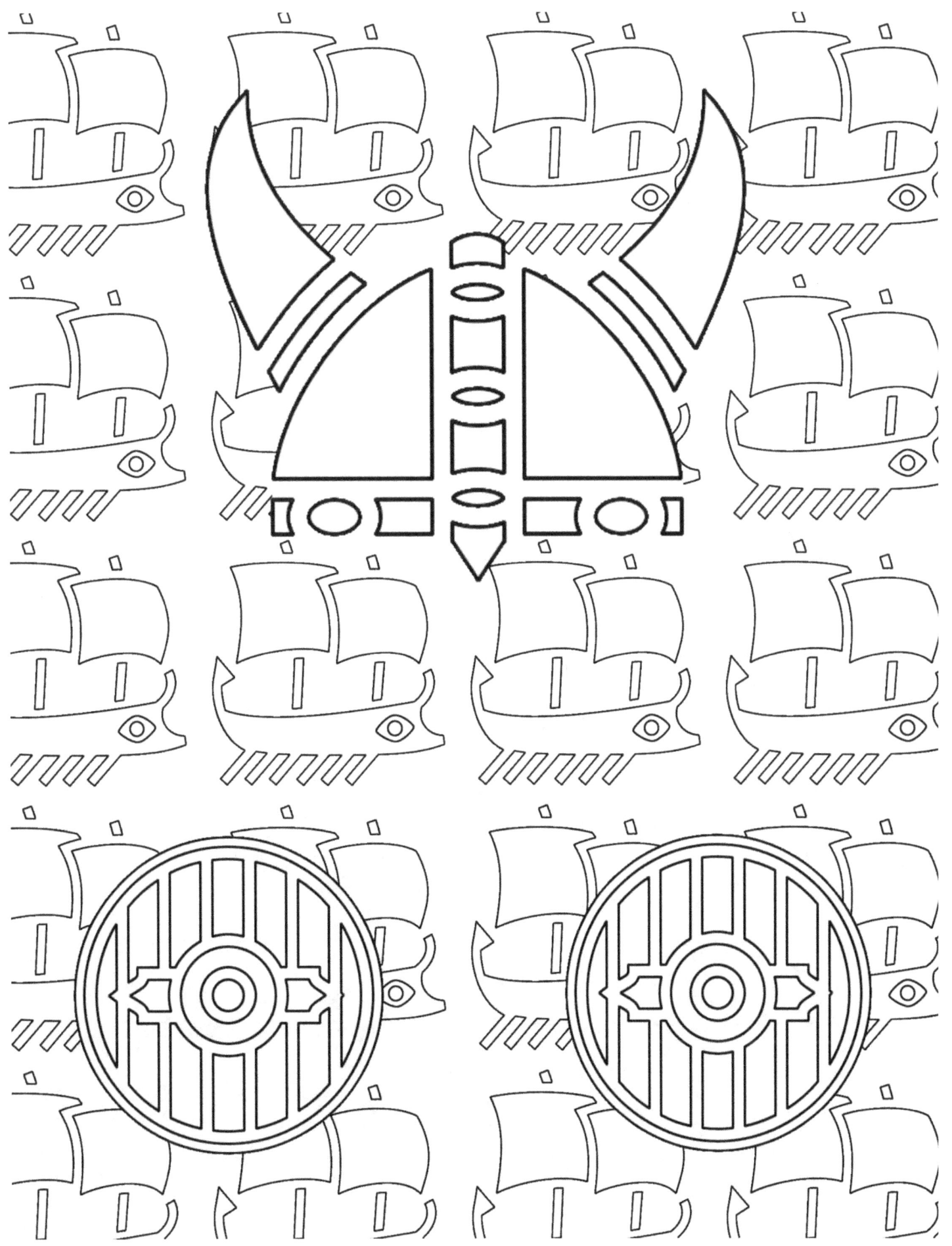

Notes

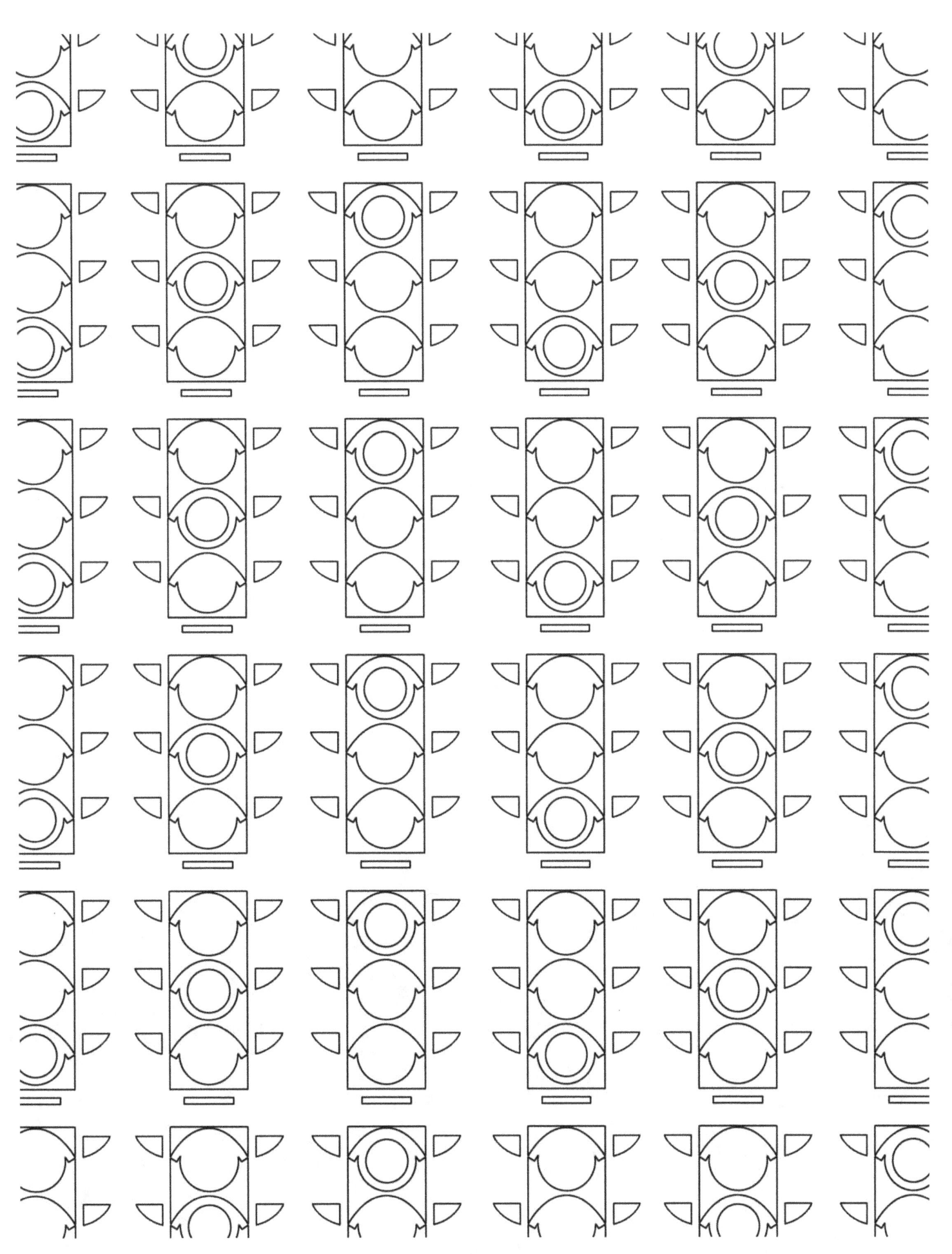

Notes

Notes

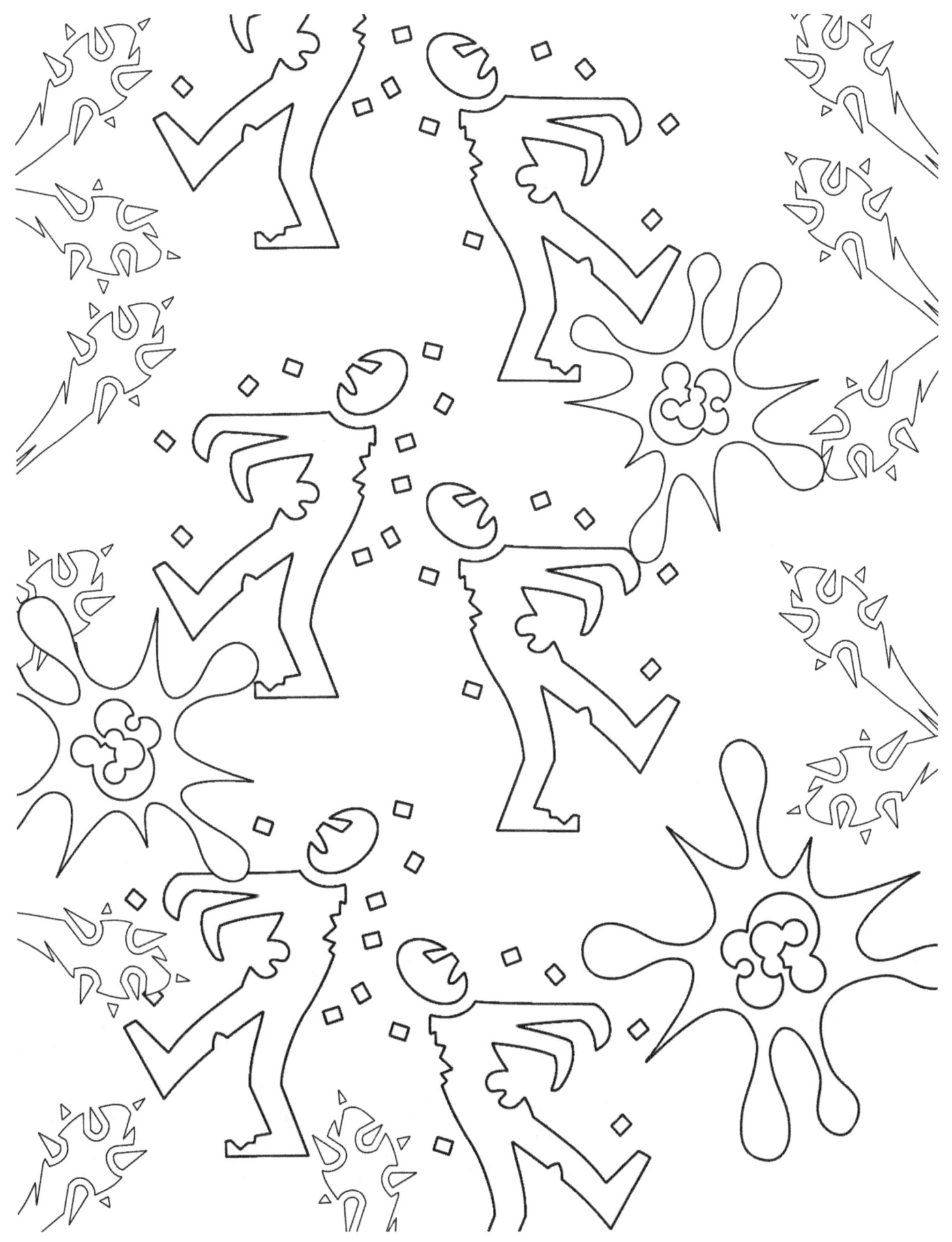

Notes

Notes

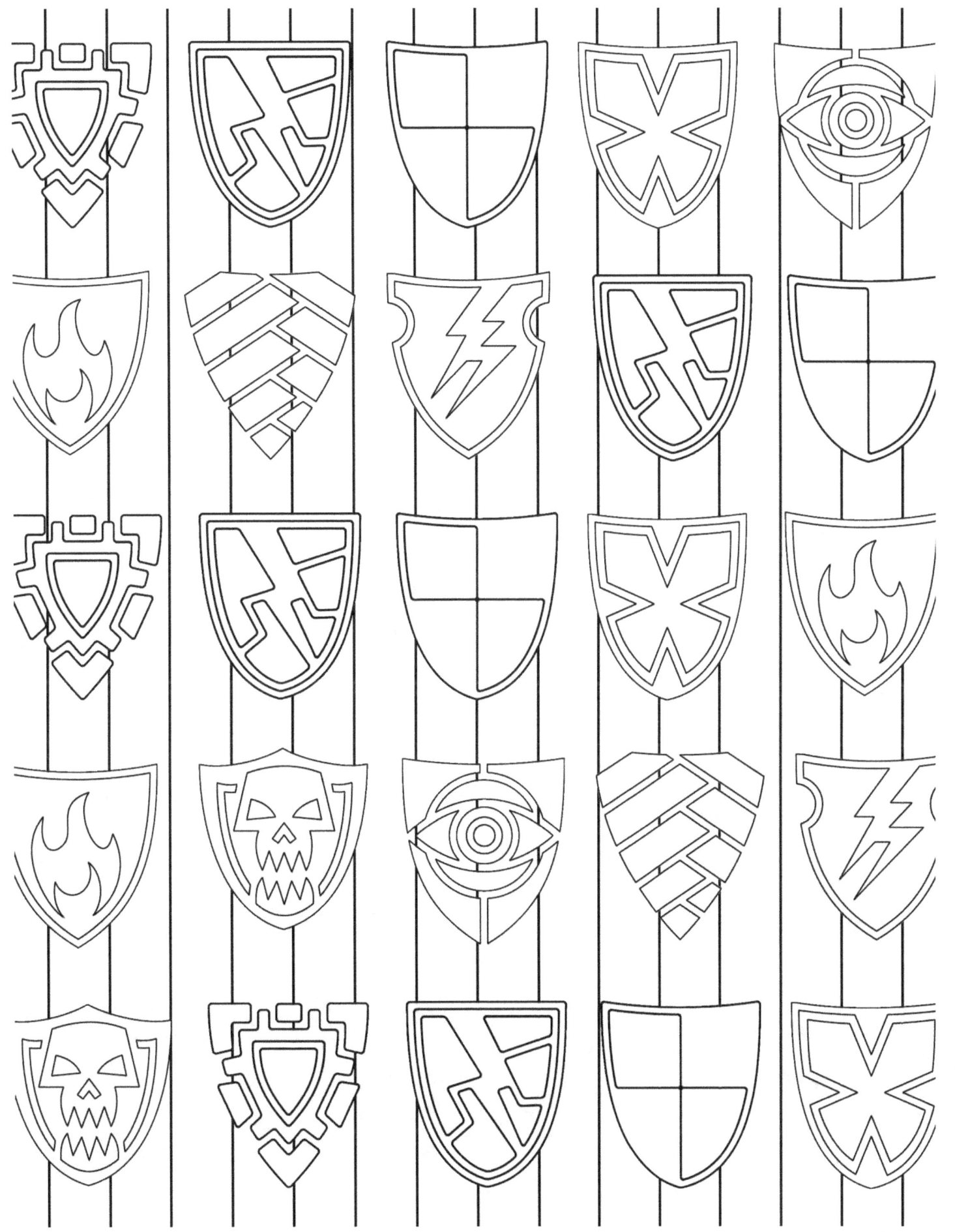

Notes

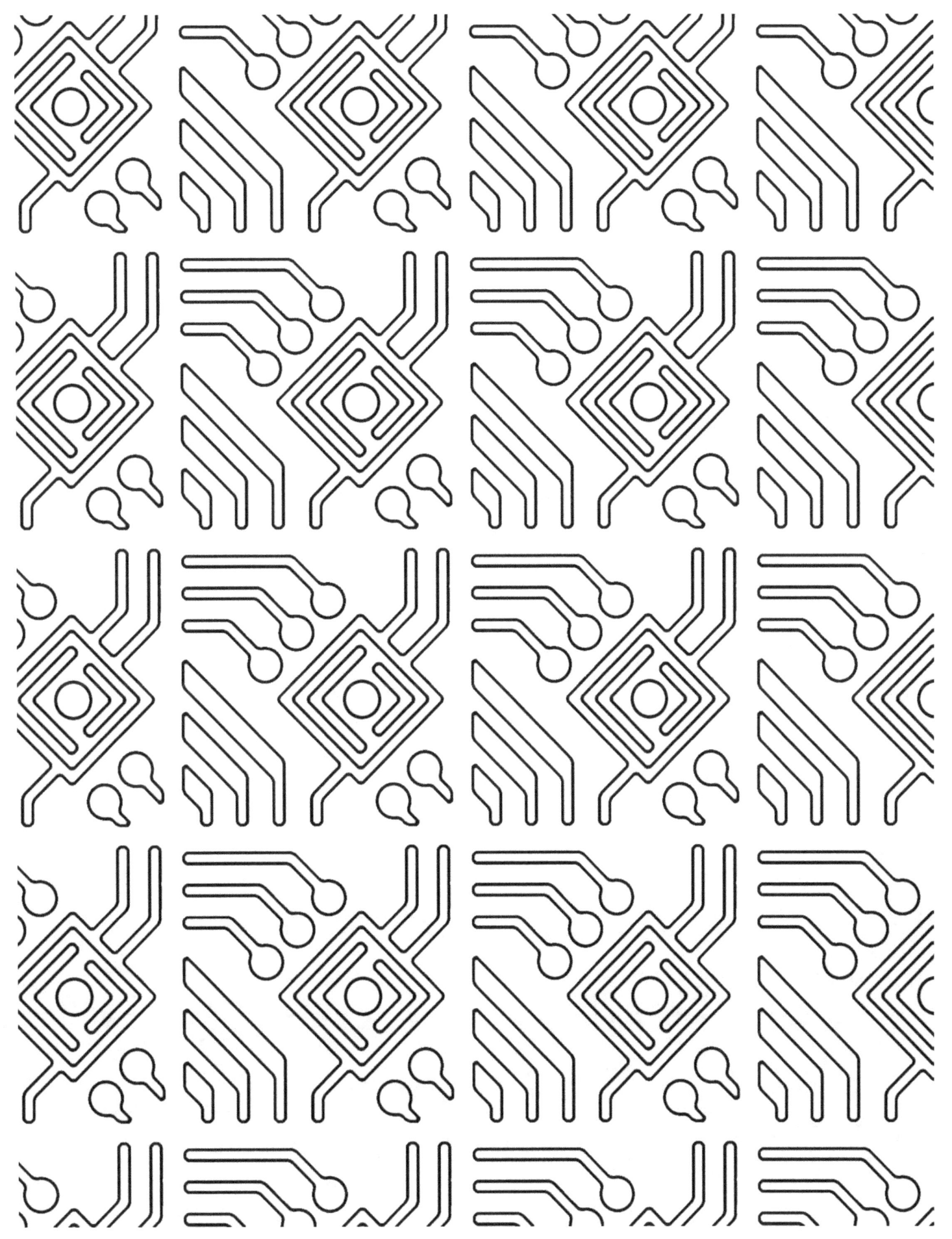

Notes

Be sure to check out these other titles by Dan Greene:

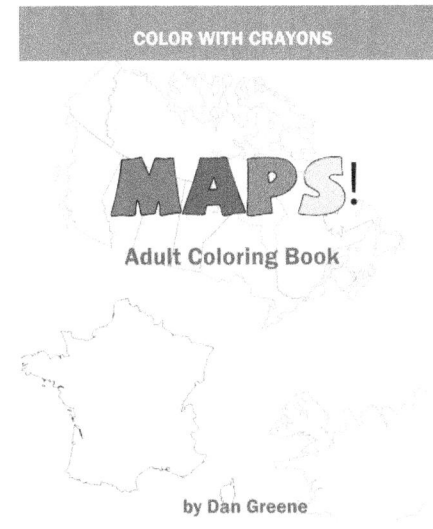

Color With Crayons: Maps!

The Big Book of Patterns

Notes